AI Income Tracking & Expense Categorization

Automated Financial Records for Smarter Tax Optimization

By Joe Correa

Published by Live Stronger Faster

This book is for educational and informational purposes only. The author and publisher are not engaged in rendering legal, financial, tax, or other professional advice. Readers should consult a qualified professional before making any financial decisions.

First Edition

Table of Contents

Introduction

Most people do not lose money on their taxes because they failed to file. They lose money because their financial records are incomplete, disorganized, or inaccurate. Income is missed, expenses are forgotten, receipts disappear, and transactions are misclassified. By the time tax season arrives, what should be a clear financial picture becomes a blurry collection of bank statements, credit card downloads, and half-remembered deductions. This chaos leads to overpaying taxes, missing legal write-offs, triggering IRS red flags, and experiencing unnecessary stress. Artificial intelligence changes this entire equation by transforming every dollar that flows through your life into a structured, searchable, compliant financial system that works quietly in the background all year long.

In the traditional world, income tracking and expense categorization depend on human memory, manual spreadsheets, and rigid accounting software. People forget to log cash payments, mislabel business meals, fail to separate personal and business spending, and miss small recurring expenses that add up to thousands in lost deductions. Even professional bookkeepers rely on data that is often incomplete or incorrectly labeled at the source. AI does not rely on memory or manual input. It connects directly to your bank accounts, payment processors, credit cards, gig platforms, payroll systems, and investment accounts, continuously reading every transaction in real time and automatically understanding what it represents, where it came from, and how it should be treated for tax purposes.

Modern AI income tracking systems do not simply record deposits. They interpret them. When money enters your account, the AI analyzes the sender, transaction description, frequency, amount, and historical patterns to determine whether the money represents wages, freelance income, rental income, dividends, capital gains, refunds, reimbursements, or transfers. It can distinguish between taxable and non-taxable income, identify irregular payments that require special reporting, and even flag missing income streams that should be accounted for. This level of intelligence eliminates one of the most common sources of IRS audits: mismatched income reporting between what you report and what banks, platforms, and employers report.

Expense categorization is even more powerful. Every time you spend money, AI evaluates the merchant, category, description, time of day, location, and past behavior to determine whether the transaction qualifies as food, travel, office supplies, education, advertising, medical expenses, home office, mileage, utilities, or dozens of other tax-relevant categories. Over time, the AI learns your habits and becomes more precise, automatically splitting mixed-use purchases into deductible and non-deductible portions. A single purchase at a big-box store can be divided into office supplies, personal groceries, and business equipment with no human intervention, creating perfect tax records that would be impossible to maintain manually.

The most valuable feature of AI-powered categorization is its ability to preserve documentation. When you take a photo of a receipt, forward an email invoice, or make an online purchase, the AI links the document to the transaction, tags it with the correct category, and stores it in a searchable digital archive. This means every deduction is supported by verifiable proof that can be instantly produced if the IRS ever asks. Instead of scrambling through shoeboxes, inboxes, and cloud folders, your entire financial life becomes a clean, audit-ready database that updates itself continuously.

AI also solves one of the biggest hidden problems in tax management: timing. Traditional accounting systems often lag weeks or months behind reality, making it impossible to know where you truly stand. AI systems operate in real time. You can see your income, expenses, profit, and tax exposure updated daily. This allows you to make smarter financial decisions throughout the year, such as accelerating expenses, delaying income, increasing retirement contributions, or adjusting withholding before problems arise. You stop reacting to taxes and start controlling them.

Another major advantage is consistency. Human bookkeeping is subjective. One month a meal might be classified as personal, the next as business. One accountant may treat a purchase differently than another. AI applies the same rules every time based on IRS guidelines, historical data, and real-time regulatory updates. This consistency reduces errors, improves compliance, and dramatically lowers audit risk. The IRS is far more likely to challenge returns that show inconsistent patterns, mismatched categories, or unexplained fluctuations. AI creates clean, predictable, defensible records that match what financial institutions report.

For people with multiple income streams, AI becomes essential. Gig workers, freelancers, real estate investors, online sellers, creators, and investors often have money flowing from dozens of platforms into multiple accounts. Tracking this manually is nearly impossible. AI aggregates all of it into one unified financial dashboard, categorizes everything automatically, and produces tax-ready reports with no extra effort. Whether you earn from Uber, Airbnb, YouTube, crypto, Amazon, consulting, or rental properties, the AI builds a complete financial map of your life that no human could realistically maintain.

This book will show you how these systems work, how they interpret financial data, and how you can use them to create flawless tax records without becoming an accountant. You will learn how AI classifies income, how it detects deductible expenses, how it links receipts to transactions, and how it prepares your data for tax filing, audits, and long-term financial planning. You will also learn how to avoid common mistakes, such as mislabeling transfers, mixing personal and business funds, or allowing uncategorized transactions to accumulate and distort your tax picture.

By the time you finish this book, you will understand that income tracking and expense categorization are no longer tedious chores. They are automated financial intelligence systems that work 24 hours a day to protect your money. When AI manages your records, every dollar is accounted for, every deduction is captured, and every tax return becomes easier, safer, and more profitable. This is the foundation of modern tax optimization, and it is the invisible engine that allows everything else in this series to work.

Chapter 1

Why Income Tracking Is the Foundation of Every Tax Strategy

Every successful tax strategy begins with one simple truth: you cannot optimize what you cannot see. Income tracking is not just a bookkeeping task, it is the foundation of legal tax reduction, audit protection, financial clarity, and long-term wealth building. When income is tracked poorly, taxes become unpredictable, deductions become risky, and financial planning becomes guesswork. For decades, individuals and small businesses relied on bank statements, spreadsheets, and accounting software that only recorded numbers without understanding their meaning. Artificial intelligence changes that by transforming income data into structured, intelligent, and compliant financial insight.

Traditional income tracking systems treat every deposit as a number in a column. They do not know whether a payment came from a client, an employer, a tenant, an investment, a refund, or a transfer between accounts. This lack of context creates tax errors. A transfer between your checking and savings account can be mistakenly counted as income. A reimbursement from a client may be taxed even though it should not be. A crypto sale may be misclassified as ordinary income instead of capital gains. AI eliminates these mistakes by reading transaction metadata, recognizing counterparties, learning payment patterns, and applying tax logic in real time.

When AI connects to your financial accounts, it creates a live map of your money. It sees where funds come from, how often they arrive, how much they vary, and how they relate to other transactions. Over time, it learns the difference between a paycheck, a freelance invoice, a rental deposit, a dividend, a crypto exchange withdrawal, or a tax refund. This intelligence allows the system to apply the correct tax treatment automatically. Instead of relying on manual labeling at the end of the year, every dollar is properly classified the moment it arrives.

Accurate income tracking is also the first layer of audit defense. The IRS receives income data from employers, banks, payment platforms, brokerage firms, and gig platforms. When what you report does not match what those institutions report, your risk of audit rises dramatically. AI systems are designed to match your records against third-party data and flag discrepancies early. This allows you to correct mistakes before filing rather than discovering them in an audit letter months later. AI does not just record income, it verifies it. One of the most powerful benefits of AI income tracking is the ability to identify hidden tax planning opportunities. When income streams are categorized correctly, the system can determine whether income qualifies for special deductions, self-employment offsets, depreciation strategies, retirement contributions, or income shifting. For example, rental income opens the door to depreciation and cost segregation. Business income allows deductions for home office, equipment, and travel. Investment income can be optimized with capital loss harvesting. AI connects income type to tax strategy automatically.

AI also eliminates one of the biggest human problems in finance: procrastination. Most people wait until tax season to organize their income, which leads to rushed decisions and missed deductions. AI works year-round, continuously organizing and updating your financial picture. This gives you the power to plan instead of panic. You can see your projected taxes, profit, and cash flow in real time and make smarter choices months before the filing deadline arrives.

Another critical advantage is scalability. As your income grows and becomes more complex, manual tracking becomes impossible. People with multiple businesses, investments, gig work, and online platforms quickly lose control of their financial data. AI does not care how many income sources you have. It scales effortlessly, processing thousands of transactions with the same accuracy as ten. This makes it ideal for modern digital earners who operate across multiple platforms and currencies.

In this chapter, you will learn how AI builds a complete income profile, how it distinguishes taxable from non-taxable funds, how it verifies your numbers against external reporting systems, and how it feeds that data into every other tax optimization tool. Income tracking is not the boring part of taxes. It is the control center. When AI controls your income data, every other strategy becomes easier, safer, and more profitable.

"The Ledger That Never Slept"

When Daniel first started his freelance design business, money flowed in from everywhere. Clients paid through PayPal, Stripe, Venmo, and bank transfers. Some paid weekly, some monthly, some late. Daniel kept a spreadsheet, but it never matched his bank account. By the time tax season arrived, he was guessing how much he had earned and praying the numbers were close enough. Every year he owed more than expected, and every year he felt like he was being punished for not understanding his own money.

One day, after receiving yet another confusing IRS notice, Daniel decided something had to change. He signed up for an AI-powered financial tracking system. At first, he was skeptical. He had tried software before, and it never seemed to get things right. But this time was different. Within minutes of connecting his accounts, the AI began labeling every transaction with uncanny accuracy. It knew which payments were from clients, which were reimbursements, which were refunds, and which were transfers between accounts.

Over the next few weeks, Daniel watched as his financial life transformed. The AI showed him how much he earned from each client, how stable his income really was, and how much tax he would owe if nothing changed. It even flagged income he had forgotten about, small deposits from old clients and affiliate commissions that would have been easy to miss. For the first time, Daniel felt like he was seeing the truth instead of a guess.

Then something unexpected happened. The AI showed him how different types of income unlocked different tax strategies. His freelance income allowed deductions for software, internet, and home office. His stock dividends had different tax rates. His crypto trades were tracked separately with capital gains calculations. Suddenly, taxes stopped being mysterious. They became logical.

When tax season arrived, Daniel didn't panic. He simply clicked a button. Every income source was categorized, verified, and reported. There were no missing numbers, no surprises, no fear. For the first time in his adult life, he knew exactly where his money came from and where it went.

Daniel realized that the real power of AI wasn't in filing taxes. It was in giving him control. The ledger never slept. Every dollar was tracked. Every opportunity was visible. And for the first time, his financial future felt predictable instead of chaotic.

Chapter 2

How AI Turns Everyday Spending into Powerful Tax Deductions

Most people believe tax deductions are something you look for once a year, but in reality deductions are created every day by how you spend money. Every meal, mile, software subscription, utility bill, piece of equipment, and online purchase carries potential tax value. The problem is that humans are not built to track these details accurately. Receipts are lost, expenses are forgotten, and purchases that qualify for deductions are lumped together with personal spending. Artificial intelligence changes this by transforming raw spending data into structured, verified, and deductible financial records.

Traditional expense tracking relies on either manual entry or bank categories that are not designed for taxes. A restaurant charge might be labeled as "food," a hardware store purchase as "shopping," or a software subscription as "miscellaneous." None of these labels meet IRS standards. AI goes deeper. It recognizes merchants, transaction histories, spending patterns, time stamps, and user behavior to determine whether an expense qualifies as business, personal, medical, educational, travel, advertising, or investment related. It does not just record what you spent; it understands why you spent it.

AI systems continuously analyze transactions in the background, building a detailed financial fingerprint of your life. Over time, the software learns that one coffee shop is where you meet clients, while another is purely personal. It understands that your home internet is partially business, your phone bill supports your freelance work, and your vehicle is used for income-producing activities. This allows it to split expenses into deductible and non-deductible portions automatically, something most people and even accountants struggle to do correctly.

One of the most powerful features of AI expense categorization is receipt intelligence. When you scan or upload a receipt, the AI extracts line-item data, tax, merchant name, date, and category, then matches it to the corresponding transaction. It knows which items are deductible and which are not, even within the same receipt. A single grocery store trip might contain office supplies, client snacks, and personal food, and the AI can separate them without human input. This creates audit-proof documentation that far exceeds traditional bookkeeping.

AI also solves one of the most dangerous tax problems: misclassification. The IRS penalizes incorrect categories because they distort taxable income. A miscategorized expense can lead to underpayment, penalties, and audits. AI applies consistent rules across all transactions, eliminating emotional judgment and guesswork. It follows tax logic, not convenience. This creates records that match IRS expectations, reducing audit risk while maximizing legal deductions.

Another major advantage is timing optimization. Because AI tracks expenses in real time, it allows you to see your deductible spending as it happens. This gives you the power to adjust behavior before the year ends. You can accelerate purchases, delay income, or increase contributions when needed. Tax planning becomes proactive instead of reactive, and your money works harder simply because the system keeps you informed.

For self-employed workers, investors, and anyone with complex finances, AI becomes a silent tax strategist. It recognizes trends, flags missing receipts, identifies unusual spending patterns, and highlights opportunities for additional deductions. Instead of reviewing thousands of transactions at year-end, the AI builds a clean, categorized, tax-ready ledger throughout the year.

This chapter will show you how AI identifies deductible expenses, how it separates business and personal spending, how it links documentation to transactions, and how it creates the foundation for every other tax strategy. When AI manages your expenses, every dollar you spend becomes a potential tax advantage instead of a forgotten opportunity.

"The Receipt Vault"

Maria ran a growing online coaching business from her home. She traveled to conferences, met clients for coffee, paid for software, advertising, internet, and a dozen tools she could barely keep track of. Every year, her accountant asked for receipts, and every year she gave him a messy folder filled with screenshots, emails, and paper slips. He did his best, but Maria always felt she was missing deductions and paying too much.

Everything changed when she started using an AI expense tracking system. Instead of throwing receipts into a folder, she simply snapped photos or forwarded emails. The AI read them instantly, matched them to her bank transactions, and filed them into the correct tax categories. Within weeks, Maria could see exactly how much she was spending on marketing, education, travel, meals, and equipment.

One day, the AI showed her something surprising. It had split her home internet and phone bill into business and personal portions based on her usage patterns. It also flagged several purchases she never realized were deductible, like cloud storage, client gifts, and part of her home utilities. Thousands of dollars she had been losing every year were now being captured automatically.

When tax season arrived, Maria didn't have to dig through anything. Every receipt, every category, every deduction was already organized and ready. Her tax bill was lower, her records were cleaner, and for the first time she felt confident instead of anxious.

Maria realized that the AI wasn't just tracking her spending. It was protecting her money. The receipt vault never forgot, never misfiled, and never missed a deduction. It quietly worked behind the scenes, turning everyday purchases into long-term financial power.

Chapter 3

How AI Creates a Living, Audit-Ready Financial Record

Once income and expenses are being tracked and categorized by artificial intelligence, something remarkable happens: your finances stop being a collection of transactions and become a living, self-updating financial record. This is far more than bookkeeping. It is a continuously evolving digital ledger that reflects not just what you earned and spent, but why, how, and under which tax rules. This living record becomes the backbone of compliance, protection, and tax optimization.

Traditional financial records are static. They are snapshots frozen in time, created weeks or months after the money moved. By the time accountants review them, errors have already been made, receipts are missing, and opportunities are lost. AI creates a dynamic financial memory. Every transaction is recorded, verified, categorized, and cross-referenced the moment it happens. If a transaction is reclassified later, the system updates the entire ledger instantly. Nothing becomes stale or outdated.

This dynamic structure is what makes AI-powered records audit-ready. The IRS does not just want totals. It wants to see the story behind the numbers. It wants to know where the money came from, why an expense was deducted, and whether documentation supports the claim. AI links every number to its source, every deduction to a receipt, and every category to a tax rule. If an auditor were to request information, the system could produce a complete, traceable explanation in seconds.

One of the most powerful features of AI-driven financial records is transaction lineage. Each dollar can be traced from its origin to its final use. Income flows into accounts, expenses flow out, and the AI understands how money moves through your financial life. This makes it nearly impossible for income to be double-counted, missed, or misclassified. Transfers between accounts are recognized. Loans are separated from income. Refunds are distinguished from revenue. This level of clarity is something human bookkeepers cannot achieve at scale.

AI also applies consistency across time. The same rules that categorize a transaction today will be applied tomorrow and next year, unless tax laws change. This creates stable patterns in your financial data that match what regulators expect. Inconsistencies are one of the biggest audit triggers. AI removes them by applying logic uniformly across all transactions, regardless of volume. Another major advantage is error detection. AI constantly scans your financial record for anomalies. If income spikes unexpectedly, expenses drop sharply, or categories suddenly change, the system flags the issue. This allows you to fix problems early instead of discovering them when it is too late. AI becomes your first line of defense against mistakes, fraud, and reporting errors.

Perhaps the most important benefit is peace of mind. When your financial record is alive and intelligent, you no longer have to fear audits, missing deductions, or IRS notices. You know that your data is clean, documented, and defensible. You can make financial decisions confidently because you are working with real numbers instead of estimates.

This chapter will show you how AI builds this living ledger, how it connects transactions to documentation, how it applies tax logic automatically, and how it transforms your financial life into a compliant, optimized, and protected system that works for you every day of the year.

"The Audit That Never Came"

Jonathan had always been afraid of the IRS. Every year, he filed his taxes and waited for the dreaded envelope in the mail. He knew his numbers were never perfect. Between his consulting work, rental income, and investments, his finances were complicated, and he always worried something was wrong. After switching to an AI-powered financial tracking system, everything changed. The software tracked every dollar he earned and spent, linked receipts to transactions, and categorized everything under tax rules he didn't even know existed. It felt like having a silent accountant working day and night.

One year, Jonathan received a letter from the IRS requesting additional information. Instead of panicking, he opened his AI dashboard. With a few clicks, he generated a full report showing income sources, expense categories, and documentation for every deduction. He uploaded it and waited.

Days passed. Then weeks. The follow-up letter never came.

Jonathan realized that the audit didn't disappear because he was lucky. It disappeared because his financial record was complete, clean, and defensible. The AI had done what humans never could. It had built a financial story that made sense.

For the first time, Jonathan didn't fear the IRS. He understood that when your ledger tells the truth, there is nothing to be afraid of.

Chapter 4

From Transactions to Intelligence: How AI Turns Records into Real-Time Tax Strategy

Once income and expenses are captured, categorized, and preserved in a living financial record, artificial intelligence moves beyond documentation and enters its most powerful role: interpretation. This is where transactions become intelligence. Numbers stop being historical artifacts and start becoming predictive signals. Traditional tax systems look backward. They summarize what already happened and calculate what you owe after the fact. AI reverses this timeline by continuously analyzing your financial activity as it occurs, transforming raw data into real-time insight that actively shapes better decisions long before tax deadlines arrive.

At the core of this transformation is pattern recognition. AI does not see transactions as isolated events. It sees relationships. It observes how income fluctuates over time, how expenses rise or fall in response, how certain categories correlate with higher tax exposure, and how changes in behavior affect projected liabilities. This allows the system to model your financial future with increasing accuracy. Instead of guessing what your tax bill might be, you can see it forming in real time, adjusted daily as money moves through your accounts.

Real-time tax intelligence fundamentally changes behavior. When people can see the tax impact of decisions immediately, they make smarter choices. AI dashboards show projected taxes owed, effective tax rates, deductible utilization, and compliance status as living metrics. This visibility turns abstract tax concepts into tangible levers. You are no longer surprised by tax bills because you have been watching them evolve all year. The fear of the unknown disappears, replaced by informed control.

AI also introduces dynamic optimization. When the system detects rising taxable income without corresponding deductions, it flags opportunities. It may suggest accelerating certain expenses, increasing retirement contributions, adjusting withholding, or reallocating spending to deductible categories where legally appropriate. These suggestions are not generic tips. They are based on your specific financial behavior, income mix, and tax profile. The system understands your thresholds and constraints, allowing it to recommend actions that fit your situation rather than one-size-fits-all advice.

Another critical function of AI-driven intelligence is scenario modeling. Because your financial record is complete and continuously updated, AI can simulate outcomes instantly. You can ask what happens if income increases, if expenses change, if a new income stream begins, or if a large purchase is made. The system recalculates projected taxes, cash flow, and compliance implications immediately. This turns tax planning into a strategic exercise rather than a guessing game.

AI also plays a vital role in preventing costly mistakes. When behavior deviates from expected patterns, the system alerts you. A sudden drop in deductible expenses, an unusual income spike, or inconsistent categorization triggers warnings. These are not punitive alerts but protective ones, designed to catch issues early while they are easy to fix. This proactive error prevention dramatically reduces audit risk and improves filing accuracy.

Perhaps the most overlooked benefit of real-time tax intelligence is emotional relief. Taxes are stressful largely because they feel uncontrollable. AI restores a sense of agency. When you know where you stand at all times, anxiety fades. You stop reacting to deadlines and start operating from a position of clarity. Taxes become another manageable system rather than a looming threat.

This chapter shows how AI transforms organized financial records into actionable intelligence, how real-time forecasting works, how optimization suggestions are generated, and how continuous awareness changes financial outcomes. When AI manages your tax intelligence, you are no longer preparing for tax season. You are living in a state of constant readiness and control.

"The Year Taxes Lost Their Power"

For most of her adult life, Evelyn believed taxes were something that happened to her, not something she could control. Every April followed the same script. She would gather documents, hand them to her accountant, wait nervously, and brace herself for the number. Sometimes it was manageable. Sometimes it hurt. But it was always a surprise. Taxes felt like a verdict handed down by a system she didn't understand.

Evelyn ran a growing online education business while managing rental income and freelance consulting on the side. Her income was strong, but unpredictable. Some months were great, others uneven. She spent money constantly on software, advertising, education, travel, and home office upgrades, yet she never felt confident that those expenses were truly helping her at tax time. She suspected she was overpaying, but she had no way to prove it.

Everything changed the year she adopted an AI-powered financial intelligence system. At first, it felt like another tool, another dashboard. But within weeks, something shifted. The AI didn't just show her transactions. It showed her meaning. It showed her projected taxes for the year based on current activity. It showed her effective tax rate adjusting as income and expenses changed. It showed her exactly how close she was to thresholds she had never even known existed.

For the first time, Evelyn could see the future forming. When income surged after a successful product launch, the AI adjusted her projected tax bill immediately. There was no panic, just awareness. When she invested in new equipment and advertising, she watched her taxable income drop in real time. The numbers told a story that made sense.

Midway through the year, the AI flagged something important. Her income had grown faster than her deductions. The system didn't scold her. It simply showed her options. Increase retirement contributions. Accelerate planned expenses. Reallocate certain subscriptions properly. Adjust quarterly payments. Each option came with projected outcomes. She could see the difference each choice would make before committing.

Evelyn began making decisions with confidence instead of fear. She timed purchases strategically. She planned growth with tax impact in mind. She stopped guessing. Taxes stopped being emotional. They became mathematical.

Then something unexpected happened. April arrived, and Evelyn felt nothing. No dread. No tension. Her tax return matched what she had been seeing all year. There were no surprises because there had been no secrets. The number felt fair, predictable, and earned.

Evelyn realized that the real power of AI wasn't saving money, although it did. It was removing uncertainty. Taxes no longer controlled her emotions or dictated her stress. She had taken the mystery out of the system, and in doing so, she had taken back control.

For the first time in her life, taxes were just another number on a screen. And that changed everything.

Chapter 5

AI for Gig Workers, Freelancers, and 1099 Income: Turning Chaos into Control

Gig workers, freelancers, and independent contractors live in a financial reality that traditional tax systems were never designed to handle. Income is inconsistent, sources multiply quickly, expenses are scattered across platforms, and tax obligations arrive without warning. Unlike W-2 employees, there is no employer withholding taxes automatically, no clean annual summary, and no safety net if something is missed. Artificial intelligence fills this gap by acting as a full-time financial intelligence layer, tracking every dollar, interpreting tax rules continuously, and transforming unpredictable income into a manageable, optimized system.

The defining challenge of 1099 income is fragmentation. A single individual may earn money from rideshare apps, freelance platforms, consulting clients, digital products, rental income, affiliate links, content monetization, and short-term contracts all at once. Each platform reports income differently, on different schedules, and sometimes inaccurately. AI solves this by aggregating all income streams into a unified system that understands how each source should be treated for tax purposes. It does not simply total deposits; it interprets them, verifies them, and reconciles them against expected third-party reporting.

Expense tracking is even more critical for gig workers because deductions are the primary tool for reducing tax burden. Without accurate categorization, freelancers often overpay thousands of dollars per year. AI identifies deductible expenses automatically, separating business from personal spending with precision that manual systems cannot achieve. Mileage, home office use, phone bills, internet, subscriptions, equipment, education, meals, travel, and advertising are continuously tracked and categorized in real time, creating a living deduction engine that operates all year.

One of the most powerful features of AI for 1099 workers is quarterly tax intelligence. Instead of waiting until April to discover a large balance due, AI projects tax obligations continuously. It estimates self-employment tax, federal income tax, and state liabilities based on current activity. This allows gig workers to set aside the correct amount of money, adjust spending, and avoid penalties. Taxes stop being a surprise and become a predictable, planned outcome. AI also protects freelancers from one of the most common mistakes in the gig economy: misclassification of income and expenses. Transfers between accounts, reimbursements, refunds, and platform fees are automatically recognized and treated correctly. This prevents overreporting income and underreporting deductions, two errors that dramatically increase tax burden and audit risk. AI enforces consistency and compliance without requiring the user to understand every rule.

Beyond compliance, AI empowers growth. When freelancers can see which income streams are most profitable after taxes, they can focus their energy strategically. AI shows net income, not just gross earnings, revealing which gigs truly build wealth and which simply create busy work. This insight allows independent workers to scale intelligently instead of blindly chasing revenue.

This chapter shows how AI transforms freelance finances from reactive chaos into proactive control. It explains how income is tracked across platforms, how deductions are captured automatically, how quarterly taxes are forecasted, and how gig workers regain financial confidence. AI does not just simplify taxes for freelancers. It gives them the clarity and control traditionally reserved for large corporations.

"1099 and Free"

For nearly a decade, Marcus told himself that freedom was worth the stress. He worked as a freelance videographer, picking up projects wherever he could find them. Weddings, corporate promos, social media content, short documentaries, online courses, real estate walkthroughs—if someone needed a camera, Marcus showed up. Money flowed in constantly, but never predictably. Some months felt abundant. Others felt terrifying.

Tax season was always the worst. Marcus avoided thinking about it until he couldn't anymore. He gathered PayPal statements, Venmo logs, Stripe exports, bank deposits, and handwritten notes, then handed them to his accountant with an apology. The result was always the same. A tax bill larger than expected and a quiet feeling that something was wrong, but impossible to pinpoint.

Marcus wasn't irresponsible. He worked harder than most people he knew. But the system wasn't built for him. No one withheld taxes. No one told him what to save. No one showed him how to track expenses properly. He lived in constant uncertainty, even when he was earning good money.

The turning point came after one particularly brutal April. Marcus owed more than he had saved, again. Sitting in his car after leaving the accountant's office, he felt something break. Not panic—clarity. He realized the problem wasn't his income. It was his lack of visibility. That week, Marcus adopted an

AI-powered financial system designed for freelancers. At first, he expected disappointment. He had tried apps before. But within days, he saw something he had never seen in his life: his entire financial picture, clean and organized, updating in real time.

The AI connected to every platform he used. It identified which deposits were client payments and which were transfers. It recognized platform fees automatically. It categorized expenses he had never properly tracked before. Gas, equipment, software, subscriptions, education, phone usage, internet, travel—it was all there, clearly labeled and documented.

Then came the moment that changed everything. The system showed him his projected taxes for the year based on his current income and expenses. The number wasn't scary. It was honest. And for the first time, Marcus understood what he needed to do. Save this much. Spend intentionally. Plan ahead.

As the months passed, Marcus stopped fearing money. He knew where he stood. When a big project landed, he saw the tax impact instantly. When expenses increased, he watched taxable income drop. The mystery was gone.

By the time April arrived again, Marcus didn't flinch. His tax bill matched what he had been seeing all year. There was no scramble, no panic, no shame. Just numbers that made sense.

Sitting at his desk after filing, Marcus smiled. He was still a freelancer. Still independent. Still free. But now, for the first time, he was 1099 and free in every sense of the word.

Chapter 6

AI for Real Estate, Crypto, and Investment Taxes: Mastering Complexity Without Fear

Real estate, cryptocurrency, and investment income represent the most misunderstood and mishandled areas of personal taxation. They are also the areas where mistakes are most expensive. Unlike wages or freelance income, investment-related taxes are governed by layered rules involving timing, classification, depreciation, holding periods, cost basis, and reporting thresholds. Traditional tax tools struggle with this complexity because they were built for static income, not dynamic assets. Artificial intelligence changes this by continuously tracking asset behavior, transaction history, and tax implications as they evolve over time.

Real estate taxation alone introduces a level of complexity that overwhelms most individuals. Rental income must be tracked separately from personal income. Expenses must be categorized correctly and allocated across properties. Depreciation schedules stretch across decades. Improvements must be distinguished from repairs. Passive activity rules apply differently depending on income levels and participation. AI systems are uniquely suited for this environment because they treat properties as living financial entities rather than static line items. Each property becomes its own ecosystem, with income, expenses, depreciation, and tax impact tracked continuously.

AI tracks rental income as it arrives, identifies platform fees, separates security deposits from taxable income, and recognizes reimbursements correctly. It categorizes expenses automatically, assigning them to the correct property and expense type. Maintenance, utilities, insurance, property management fees, travel, supplies, and professional services are all classified under tax-appropriate categories. Depreciation is calculated automatically using IRS-approved methods, adjusted when improvements occur, and reflected in real-time tax projections. This eliminates one of the most common and costly errors in real estate taxation: underutilized or incorrectly applied depreciation.

Cryptocurrency introduces an entirely different layer of complexity. Unlike traditional assets, crypto transactions can generate taxable events even without cash changing hands. Trades, swaps, staking rewards, mining income, airdrops, and transfers all carry potential tax consequences. Many investors mistakenly believe taxes only apply when crypto is converted to fiat, leading to severe underreporting. AI solves this by tracking every transaction across wallets, exchanges, and blockchains, calculating cost basis, holding periods, and gains or losses automatically.

AI also excels at reconciling fragmented crypto data. Investors often use multiple wallets and exchanges, each with incomplete reporting. AI aggregates this data into a unified ledger, identifying transfers versus trades and preventing double-counting. It calculates short-term and long-term capital gains accurately and applies the correct tax treatment based on jurisdiction and timing. This level of precision is nearly impossible to achieve manually and is increasingly critical as regulators increase scrutiny of digital assets.

Investment income from stocks, bonds, dividends, and funds adds yet another dimension. Dividends may be qualified or non-qualified. Capital gains depend on holding periods. Losses can be harvested strategically. Wash sale rules complicate reporting. AI continuously monitors investment activity, categorizes income correctly, and identifies tax optimization opportunities such as loss harvesting or timing adjustments. Instead of reacting to gains at year-end, investors can plan strategically throughout the year.

The true power of AI emerges when these asset classes intersect. A single individual may earn rental income, trade crypto, receive dividends, and sell assets in the same year. AI integrates all of this activity into a unified tax intelligence system, ensuring consistency, compliance, and optimization across the entire portfolio. It shows how one decision affects another, allowing for coordinated tax planning rather than isolated guesses.

This chapter explains how AI manages real estate depreciation, crypto transactions, investment income classification, and cross-asset tax optimization. It shows how complexity becomes manageable when intelligence replaces manual effort. With AI, even the most advanced investment strategies can be executed confidently, accurately, and legally.

"The Investor Who Finally Slept"

For years, Thomas told himself he understood money. He owned rental properties, traded stocks, and invested early in cryptocurrency. On paper, he was successful. But beneath the surface, he lived with constant unease. Every financial decision felt like a gamble, not because of market risk, but because of taxes. He never truly knew what a decision would cost him until it was too late.

Thomas owned three rental properties in different states. He tracked income and expenses in spreadsheets that never quite balanced. Depreciation was something his accountant "handled," but Thomas didn't understand how. He traded stocks frequently, sometimes holding for months, sometimes for days. Crypto was even worse. He had wallets everywhere, exchanges he barely remembered signing up for, and transactions he didn't fully understand. At night, he wondered how much of this the IRS could see.

Tax season was unbearable. Thomas would sit across from his accountant, answering questions he didn't fully understand, signing returns he hoped were correct. The numbers were always large. The explanations were always vague. He felt successful but strangely powerless.

Everything changed after a conversation with another investor who seemed calm in a way Thomas wasn't. When Thomas asked him how he managed taxes with so many assets, the man smiled and said, "I don't manage them. My system does."

Skeptical but desperate, Thomas adopted an AI-powered financial intelligence platform. The onboarding process alone revealed how fragmented his financial life had been. The AI connected to his bank accounts, brokerage accounts, crypto exchanges, and rental platforms. Within days, it had built a complete map of his financial universe.

The first shock was clarity. Each rental property appeared as its own profile. Income, expenses, depreciation, and net cash flow were visible instantly. The AI showed Thomas how much depreciation he had been missing and how certain expenses had been misallocated for years. Crypto transactions were reconstructed across wallets, revealing gains and losses he hadn't known existed. Stock trades were categorized by holding period, showing the true tax cost of his trading habits.

Then came understanding. The AI didn't just show numbers. It showed relationships. When Thomas considered selling a property, the system projected depreciation recapture and capital gains. When he thought about trading crypto, it showed short-term versus long-term implications. When markets dipped, it identified opportunities to harvest losses strategically.

For the first time, Thomas felt like an owner instead of a gambler. Decisions became deliberate. Taxes became predictable. Complexity became manageable.

One night, months later, Thomas noticed something unexpected. He was sleeping. Deeply. Without running scenarios in his head. Without fearing letters in the mail. The system was watching when he wasn't. It was calculating when he couldn't. It was protecting him silently.

Thomas realized that wealth isn't just about making money. It's about understanding it. And for the first time, he truly did.

Chapter 7

AI Tax Forecasting & Withholding Optimization: Eliminating Surprises Before They Exist

Tax forecasting is the difference between reacting to taxes and controlling them. For most people, taxes are experienced as a once-a-year shock, a number revealed long after decisions have already been made. Income has been earned, money has been spent, and opportunities to adjust have passed. Artificial intelligence eliminates this delayed feedback loop by turning tax planning into a continuous, real-time process that evolves alongside your financial life. Instead of asking what you owe after the year ends, AI answers a far more powerful question: where are you headed, and how can you adjust now?

Traditional tax forecasting relies on static assumptions. Accountants estimate based on prior-year returns, partial data, or averages that rarely reflect reality. These forecasts are often outdated the moment they are created. AI forecasting systems operate differently. They ingest live income and expense data, apply current tax rules, and update projections continuously. Every transaction nudges the forecast. Every decision alters the trajectory. Taxes stop being an annual event and become a measurable, manageable variable.

One of the most important benefits of AI tax forecasting is accuracy through completeness. Because AI already tracks income, expenses, deductions, depreciation, investment activity, and asset behavior, forecasts are built on real data rather than estimates. The system knows your effective tax rate, marginal brackets, self-employment obligations, capital gains exposure, and state liabilities. This allows it to project not just a single number, but a range of outcomes based on different scenarios.

Withholding optimization is where forecasting becomes action. Many people overpay taxes all year through excessive withholding or underpay and face penalties later. AI analyzes your income patterns and tax exposure to determine optimal withholding levels. For W-2 earners, it can suggest adjustments that increase cash flow without risking underpayment. For freelancers and investors, it calculates precise quarterly payments that align with actual earnings rather than rough guesses. This keeps money working for you instead of sitting idle with the government.

AI also adapts to change. When income rises unexpectedly, forecasts adjust immediately. When deductions increase, projected liabilities drop. When laws change, calculations update automatically. This responsiveness is critical in modern financial lives where income streams shift rapidly. AI ensures that your tax strategy evolves as fast as your reality does.

Another powerful feature is scenario planning. AI allows you to explore what-if questions without consequences. What happens if income increases by 20 percent? What if you sell an asset? What if you increase retirement contributions? What if you change filing status or move states? The system recalculates outcomes instantly, allowing you to make decisions with full visibility into their tax impact. This turns tax planning into a strategic exercise rather than a guessing game.

Perhaps the most profound impact of AI forecasting is psychological. Tax anxiety thrives in uncertainty. When people don't know what to expect, they assume the worst. AI removes this fear by replacing uncertainty with clarity. You know where you stand. You know where you are going. You know what to do if adjustments are needed. This confidence changes behavior, encouraging smarter decisions and reducing financial stress.

This chapter explains how AI builds accurate tax forecasts, how withholding optimization works, how quarterly payments are calculated, and how scenario modeling empowers proactive decision-making. When AI manages forecasting, tax season loses its power to surprise, intimidate, or disrupt your financial life.

"The Year There Were No Surprises"

For as long as she could remember, Natalie associated success with anxiety. As her career grew, so did her income, and with it came an ever-present sense of dread about taxes. She earned well, invested aggressively, and saved diligently, yet every April felt like walking into an exam she hadn't studied for. No matter how prepared she thought she was, the number was always different than expected.

Natalie was disciplined. She tracked spending. She hired professionals. She did everything she was told. But the system still felt adversarial. She never knew how much money was truly hers because taxes always lingered in the background, undefined and unpredictable.

The breaking point came one year after an unexpectedly large tax bill wiped out most of her savings cushion. She hadn't underreported income or made reckless decisions. She had simply earned more than anticipated and hadn't adjusted in time. Sitting at her kitchen table late one night, Natalie realized the problem wasn't her behavior. It was the delay. She was always learning the truth too late. That was the year she adopted an AI-powered tax forecasting system. At first, it felt almost unsettling. The dashboard showed her projected tax liability for the year, updated daily. It wasn't a guess. It was built on everything she was actually earning and spending. For the first time, she could see the road ahead instead of just the rearview mirror.

When she received a bonus, the projection adjusted instantly. When investment income fluctuated, the system recalculated. When she made deductible purchases, the numbers responded in real time. Nothing was hidden. Nothing was delayed.

Then came the moment that changed how Natalie thought about money. The AI alerted her that her withholding was too high. She had been overpaying taxes all year, sending thousands of dollars to the government unnecessarily. The system showed her exactly how to adjust, how much cash flow it would free up, and why it was safe. She made the change.

Months passed, and something strange happened. Natalie stopped worrying. Not because she didn't care, but because she knew. When friends complained about tax season approaching, she felt detached, almost calm. She had been watching her tax position evolve all year. There were no mysteries left.

When April arrived, Natalie filed her return without emotion. The final number matched the projection she had been seeing for months. No shock. No panic. No regret. Later that evening, she sat quietly, reflecting on how different the year had felt. It wasn't just the money. It was the absence of fear. The absence of uncertainty. The sense that she was finally ahead of the system instead of chasing it.

Natalie realized something profound. Wealth isn't just about earning more. It's about removing surprises. And for the first time in her life, there were none.

Chapter 8

AI Tax Law, Compliance, and Filing Rules: Staying Aligned in a World That Never Stops Changing

Tax law is not static. It shifts constantly, shaped by legislation, court rulings, regulatory updates, enforcement priorities, and political agendas. For the average taxpayer, this creates an impossible challenge. Rules change faster than most people can learn them, and ignorance is never an acceptable defense. Artificial intelligence solves this problem by acting as a continuously updating compliance engine, ensuring that your financial activity remains aligned with current tax law without requiring you to monitor every change yourself.

Traditional tax compliance depends on delayed updates. Software updates once a year. Accountants learn new rules after they are enacted. Taxpayers discover changes only when something goes wrong. AI operates on a different timeline. It monitors regulatory updates in real time, integrates new rules into its decision-making logic, and applies them instantly to your financial data. This means compliance is no longer a year-end concern but a continuous state. One of the most critical aspects of compliance is classification. Tax law is built on definitions. What counts as income, what qualifies as a deduction, how assets are treated, and when taxes are triggered all depend on precise categorization. AI applies these definitions consistently across every transaction. It does not rely on memory or judgment. It follows rules. When definitions change, the system updates its logic and re-evaluates transactions accordingly, preserving accuracy across time.

Filing rules add another layer of complexity. Deadlines differ based on income type, filing status, entity structure, and jurisdiction. Reporting thresholds vary. Forms change. Disclosure requirements expand. AI tracks these variables automatically, ensuring that required forms are prepared, deadlines are met, and disclosures are complete. This reduces one of the most common sources of penalties: missing or incorrect filings rather than incorrect calculations.

AI also protects against over-compliance, an often overlooked problem. Many taxpayers pay more than required out of fear. They avoid deductions, over-withhold, or delay strategies because they are unsure what is allowed. AI removes this fear by applying rules precisely. It maximizes what is legal while staying firmly within compliance boundaries. This balance is difficult for humans to maintain but natural for rule-based intelligence systems. Another key advantage of AI-driven compliance is audit readiness. Compliance is not just about following rules; it is about being able to prove that you did. AI maintains detailed logs showing how each decision was made, which rules were applied, and what documentation supports each position. If questioned, the system can produce a complete compliance trail that demonstrates good-faith adherence to the law.

As governments modernize enforcement and increase data matching, compliance will only become more important. AI aligns your financial records with how regulators think, report, and verify information. It ensures consistency between what you report and what institutions report about you. This alignment dramatically reduces risk while increasing confidence.

This chapter explains how AI tracks legal changes, applies compliance logic, manages filing rules, and preserves audit-ready documentation automatically. When AI handles compliance, you no longer need to chase rules. The system moves with the law so you can focus on living and building instead of worrying.

"The Quiet Confidence of Being Right"

For most of his life, Robert followed the rules because he was afraid of breaking them. He filed on time, paid what he was told, and avoided anything that felt complicated. Taxes were not something he wanted to understand deeply. They were something he wanted to survive.

Robert owned a small consulting firm that had grown steadily over the years. With growth came complexity. New income streams. New deductions. New reporting requirements. Each year, his accountant asked more questions. Each year, Robert felt less certain that he was doing things correctly. He wasn't trying to cheat the system, but he didn't trust it either.

The fear wasn't dramatic. It was quiet. A low-level tension that followed him into every financial decision. Should he deduct this? Should he report that differently? Is this still allowed? The rules seemed to change constantly, and Robert felt like he was always one step behind.

One year, after receiving a confusing notice about a filing requirement he didn't even know existed, Robert decided he needed a different approach. Not more effort, but more certainty. That's when he adopted an AI-powered tax compliance system.

At first, he expected complexity. Instead, he found calm. The system didn't overwhelm him with rules. It simply worked. Transactions were categorized automatically. Forms appeared when needed. Deadlines were flagged early. When rules changed, the system adjusted quietly in the background.

Over time, Robert noticed something subtle but profound. His fear began to fade. Not because he cared less, but because he trusted more. The AI didn't guess. It didn't forget. It didn't apply rules inconsistently. It followed the law exactly as written, updated as needed, without emotion.

One afternoon, Robert found himself considering a deduction he would have avoided in the past. Instead of hesitating, he checked the system. It showed him the rule, the justification, and the documentation. The decision was no longer emotional. It was factual.

Months later, during a routine review, his accountant paused. "Your records are exceptionally clean," she said. "Everything aligns perfectly." Robert felt a wave of relief he hadn't realized he was missing.

That night, sitting quietly at home, Robert reflected on the change. He hadn't become more aggressive or careless. He had become precise. The fear was gone, replaced by confidence grounded in clarity.

Robert realized that compliance doesn't have to feel restrictive. When done correctly, it feels liberating. The rules stop being something you fear and become something you understand. And in that understanding, there is peace.

For the first time in years, Robert wasn't hoping he was right. He knew he was.

Chapter 9

AI Financial Planning & Wealth Protection: Where Taxes, Assets, and the Future Align

At the highest level, taxes are not an isolated obligation. They are a force that touches every financial decision you make across your lifetime. Income, spending, investing, saving, retiring, gifting, and protecting assets are all interconnected through tax rules. When these areas are managed separately, people lose money, miss opportunities, and create unnecessary risk. Artificial intelligence changes this by unifying tax intelligence with long-term financial planning, transforming scattered decisions into a coordinated strategy designed to protect and grow wealth over time.

Traditional financial planning often treats taxes as an afterthought. Advisors project returns, recommend investments, and suggest retirement strategies, then adjust for taxes later. This approach is backward. Taxes shape net outcomes more than market performance alone. AI flips the model by placing tax intelligence at the center of planning. Every recommendation is evaluated based on after-tax impact, not just gross performance. This ensures that growth strategies are realistic, sustainable, and aligned with real-world outcomes.

AI-powered financial planning begins with a complete understanding of your financial ecosystem. Income streams, assets, liabilities, tax brackets, deductions, credits, depreciation schedules, and investment behavior are all integrated into a single model. This allows AI to forecast not just next year's taxes, but how today's decisions will affect your financial position five, ten, or twenty years into the future. Retirement contributions, asset sales, inheritance planning, and income timing are evaluated holistically instead of in isolation.

Wealth protection is where this intelligence becomes especially powerful. Taxes are one of the greatest threats to long-term wealth, yet they are often invisible until damage has already been done. AI identifies strategies to legally reduce exposure over time, such as tax-efficient asset placement, timing of income recognition, strategic use of deductions, and coordination between taxable, tax-deferred, and tax-free accounts. These decisions compound quietly, creating meaningful differences over decades.

AI also helps manage risk. Market volatility, regulatory change, and life events can disrupt even the best-laid plans.

Because AI systems continuously update projections and assumptions, they can adapt strategies dynamically. If income changes, markets shift, or laws evolve, the system recalibrates. This flexibility is critical in a world where long-term certainty is rare. AI planning is not rigid. It is resilient.

Another crucial benefit is clarity across life stages. Early in life, AI may emphasize growth, reinvestment, and deduction optimization. In mid-career, it may focus on income smoothing, asset diversification, and liability management. Later, it prioritizes withdrawal strategies, tax-efficient distributions, and legacy planning. The system evolves as you do, ensuring that financial decisions remain aligned with your goals and realities.

Perhaps most importantly, AI restores intentionality. Instead of reacting to taxes, market swings, or deadlines, you act with purpose. Decisions are informed by long-term impact rather than short-term pressure. Financial planning becomes less about prediction and more about preparation.

This chapter explains how AI integrates tax intelligence with wealth planning, how it protects assets across time, how it coordinates retirement and investment strategies, and how it turns financial uncertainty into structured confidence. When

AI manages planning, money becomes a tool for living well rather than a source of constant concern.

"The Long View"

When Daniel turned fifty, he didn't feel old, but he felt something shift. Time began to feel heavier, more valuable. He had spent decades building a successful career, investing diligently, and saving responsibly. On paper, he was doing everything right. Yet beneath the surface, a quiet question followed him everywhere: Is this enough? Not just the money, but the plan.

Daniel had always treated taxes as something separate from life. He paid them, minimized them where possible, and moved on. Retirement planning was something he assumed would work itself out if he saved enough. Wealth protection meant insurance and diversification. These were all boxes to check, not parts of a single system.

The moment that changed everything came during a routine financial review. Daniel asked a simple question: "What does my future actually look like after taxes?" The room went quiet. His advisors spoke in estimates, assumptions, and probabilities. No one could give him a clear answer. That uncertainty stayed with him.

That year, Daniel adopted an AI-powered financial planning system that integrated tax intelligence into every projection. At first, the information felt overwhelming. The system showed him not just balances, but trajectories. How his income would taper. How withdrawals would be taxed. How investment choices would affect his lifestyle decades later. It was the first time anyone had shown him the full picture.

What surprised Daniel most wasn't the numbers. It was the patterns. The AI revealed how small tax decisions compounded over time. How delaying certain strategies had cost him more than market downturns ever did. How adjusting income timing could dramatically improve his retirement security. These weren't dramatic changes. They were subtle, disciplined shifts applied consistently.

As months passed, Daniel began to think differently. He stopped asking, "How much can I make?" and started asking, "How much can I keep?" He coordinated his investments with tax strategy. He planned withdrawals years in advance. He stopped reacting to market noise and focused on long-term alignment.

One evening, sitting quietly at home, Daniel reviewed a projection that stretched thirty years into the future. It wasn't perfect. Nothing ever is. But it was clear. Sustainable. Intentional. He could see how he would live, not just survive.

For the first time, Daniel felt calm about the future. Not because it was guaranteed, but because it was designed. His money had a purpose beyond accumulation. It supported his life, his values, and his peace of mind.

Daniel realized that wealth isn't about numbers on a screen. It's about confidence across time. And with the long view finally visible, he knew he was ready for whatever came next.

Chapter 10

The Future of AI-Powered Personal Taxes: Automated Filing, Digital IRS, and Zero-Stress Compliance

The future of personal taxation will not be defined by new forms, higher rates, or more complicated rules. It will be defined by intelligence. As governments digitize enforcement and financial systems become increasingly interconnected, the traditional tax model—manual preparation, annual filing anxiety, and reactive compliance—will become obsolete. Artificial intelligence is not merely improving the tax process; it is redesigning it entirely. In the future, taxes will be continuous, automated, predictive, and largely invisible to the individual.

AI-powered tax systems are already shifting taxation away from annual events toward real-time alignment. Instead of summarizing a year after it ends, AI systems continuously reconcile income, expenses, assets, and obligations as they occur. This eliminates the lag that creates stress, errors, and penalties. Taxes become an always-current state rather than a once-a-year reckoning. The concept of "tax season" begins to fade, replaced by ongoing accuracy. Automated filing is a natural outcome of this evolution. When income, expenses, deductions, credits, depreciation, investments, and compliance are tracked continuously under current law, filing becomes a formality rather than a task. AI systems already generate tax-ready returns dynamically. In the near future, filing will simply mean authorizing submission. The human role shifts from calculation to oversight, from labor to confirmation.

As tax authorities modernize, AI will align seamlessly with digital IRS systems. Governments are moving toward pre-filled returns, data matching, and automated verification. AI-powered personal tax systems are designed to operate in this environment. They ensure consistency between what individuals report and what institutions report about them. This alignment dramatically reduces disputes, audits, and enforcement actions. Compliance becomes collaborative rather than adversarial.

Zero-stress taxation does not mean zero responsibility. It means responsibility supported by intelligence. AI does not remove accountability; it strengthens it by ensuring accuracy, documentation, and transparency. When systems operate continuously and intelligently, mistakes become rare, intentional misreporting becomes harder, and good-faith compliance becomes easier than avoidance. The future also brings personalization. AI tax systems will adapt to individual lives, careers, and goals. They will recognize life events—marriage, children, career changes, investments, relocations—and adjust strategies accordingly. Taxes will no longer be generic calculations but personalized financial pathways optimized for each individual's reality.

Ethics and trust will play a critical role. As AI takes on more responsibility, transparency becomes essential. Systems must explain decisions, show logic, and preserve human oversight. The future of AI-powered taxes is not blind automation but informed partnership between humans and machines.

This final chapter shows how AI transforms taxation from stress into structure, from fear into clarity, and from obligation into alignment. The future of taxes is not about paying less or more. It is about paying correctly, confidently, and without disruption to life.

"The Last Tax Season"

Eleanor remembered the sound of paper. The rustle of envelopes, the scratch of pens, the quiet dread that arrived every spring. Taxes had always marked time for her. Not by dates, but by emotions. Stress. Uncertainty. Relief. Regret. For most of her adult life, taxes felt like a test she never quite studied for, no matter how responsible she tried to be. Eleanor wasn't careless. She worked steadily, saved diligently, invested thoughtfully. But every April carried the same weight. She gathered documents, answered questions, waited for numbers she couldn't predict. Sometimes the outcome was fine. Sometimes it wasn't. The unpredictability was exhausting.

As technology advanced, Eleanor watched the world change around her. Banking became digital. Investing became automated. Communication became instant. Yet taxes remained stubbornly archaic in her mind, anchored to forms, deadlines, and anxiety.

That began to change the year she adopted an AI-powered tax system—not because she was struggling, but because she was tired. Tired of uncertainty. Tired of reacting. Tired of feeling like something so fundamental should be so disruptive.

At first, the system felt almost too quiet. There were no alarms, no urgent prompts. Just clarity. Income was tracked automatically. Expenses were categorized instantly. Compliance updated silently as laws changed. Eleanor could see her tax position at any moment, not as a threat, but as information.

Months passed, and something strange happened. Eleanor stopped thinking about taxes. Not because she was avoiding them, but because there was nothing to think about. The system worked continuously, adjusting as life unfolded. When she earned more, projections updated. When she invested, implications were visible. When rules changed, compliance adapted.

One afternoon, Eleanor realized she hadn't worried about April in months. The thought startled her. Taxes had always lived in the back of her mind, a low-level hum of concern. Now there was silence.

When filing time arrived, it barely registered. The system generated her return, showed her the logic, and asked for approval. She reviewed it calmly, not with suspicion, but with understanding. The numbers matched what she had seen all year. There were no surprises because there had been no secrets.

After submitting, Eleanor sat quietly and reflected. It wasn't just that taxes had become easier. It was that they had stopped interrupting her life. They no longer dictated her mood or consumed her attention. They had become what they always should have been: a background system that worked while she lived.

Eleanor realized that this was the future she had hoped for without knowing how to name it. A future where compliance didn't require fear. Where responsibility didn't require stress.

Where intelligence carried the burden so humans didn't have to.

That year, Eleanor didn't say she survived tax season. She didn't even notice it had passed.

It was, she realized, the last tax season she would ever feel.

Final Thoughts

From Records to Results: Living in Financial Clarity

By the time you reach the end of this book, one truth should be unmistakably clear: income tracking and expense categorization are no longer administrative tasks. They are strategic advantages. In a world where money moves instantly, across platforms, borders, and asset classes, relying on memory, spreadsheets, or outdated tools is no longer just inefficient—it is financially dangerous. Artificial intelligence changes the relationship between people and their finances by replacing fragmentation with cohesion and uncertainty with clarity.

Throughout this book, you have seen how AI transforms raw transactions into structured intelligence. Income is no longer a vague total discovered at tax time; it is a living stream that can be understood, verified, and optimized in real time. Expenses are no longer forgotten receipts or vague categories; they become documented, categorized, and defensible deductions that work continuously to protect your wealth. When these systems operate together, financial records stop being historical artifacts and become decision-making tools. The deeper lesson of AI-powered financial organization is not about technology. It is about control. For generations, people have accepted financial stress as normal. They have assumed that taxes must be confusing, that audits are random threats, and that surprises are inevitable. This belief persists not because it is true, but because people have never had access to systems that operate with the same intelligence and consistency as the institutions evaluating them. AI levels that imbalance.

When your financial records are complete, consistent, and continuously updated, fear loses its grip. There is nothing left to guess, nothing left to scramble for, nothing left to hope was done correctly. Confidence replaces anxiety not because risk disappears, but because uncertainty does. This is the psychological transformation that underlies every practical benefit described in this book.

AI income tracking and expense categorization also change how people relate to growth. Instead of chasing revenue blindly, individuals can see which income streams truly produce wealth after taxes. Instead of spending reactively, they can allocate resources intentionally. Instead of waiting for professionals to interpret the past, they can shape the future themselves. This shift from reaction to intention is the hallmark of financial maturity in the AI era. As part of the larger *AI Personal Tax Optimization* series, this book serves as a foundation. Without accurate income and expense intelligence, advanced tax strategies collapse. Forecasting becomes unreliable. Compliance becomes risky. Wealth planning becomes guesswork. But when this foundation is strong, every other strategy becomes more effective, more defensible, and more powerful.

The future of personal finance does not belong to those who work the hardest or earn the most. It belongs to those who see clearly. AI provides that clarity—not by replacing human judgment, but by supporting it with precision, consistency, and scale. When intelligence handles the details, people are free to focus on living, building, and growing with confidence.

This is not the end of the journey. It is the moment when chaos gives way to structure, and structure gives way to freedom.

www.ingramcontent.com/pod-product-compliance
Lightning Source LLC
LaVergne TN
LVHW022027200926
848481LV00007B/2571

* 9 7 9 8 2 9 5 5 8 6 0 1 9 *